# A
# BOOK
# OF
# UNCOMMON
# PRAYERS

CATHERINE DE VINCK

# A
# BOOK
## OF
# UNCOMMON
# PRAYERS

ALLELUIA PRESS

*By the same author:*
– A TIME TO GATHER, Alleluia Press, 1967 and 1974
– IKON, Alleluia Press, 1972 and 1974
– A LITURGY, Cross-Currents, 1973
– A PASSION PLAY, Alleluia Press, 1975

© 1976, Catherine de Vinck
ISBN 0-911726-23-3 Cloth
ISBN 0-911726-24-1 Paperback
Library of Congress Catalog Nr. 76-44149
Designed and published by ALLELUIA PRESS,
  Box 103, Allendale, N.J. 07401
  Printed in the United States of America

To my brothers of Weston Priory
in thanksgiving
for their share in the creation of this book
and for their loving presence
in my life.

# CONTENTS

# FOREWORD

In the mysterious human activity we call prayer, there is a time for speaking and a time to listen, a time for dancing and a time to be still, a time for healing and a time to be healed. Prayer is a time of communication, a time of communion and a time of creativity.

Prayer, in the spirit of Jesus, invites us to use our best available means of communication, of communion, and of creativity. In response to this call, we are learning to sing and to dance, and to enjoy beautiful and functional space for prayer—and we are discovering that good music, graceful dance, thoughtful art and architecture are wholesome means of communication with a gracious God as well as a way to express our communion with one another.

As Christian communities in the process of integrating these elements into a more textured, intense and harmonious expression of prayer, we are faced with a particular challenge: how can we best express the contemplative dimension of our prayer? It is here that the gift of poetry presents its unique potential.

Poetry has the power to open up the "listening" of the community, of breaking up stereotyped religious understandings, of freeing and uniting a community to receive and express new meaning.

The poetry of Catherine de Vinck is one of the rare and rich resources for contemporary religious poetry available today. Original, fresh, intensely personal and yet intuitive of the social implications of the Gospel today, this poetry will speak to persons and communities who wish to develop the contemplative dimension of their prayer.

A BOOK OF UNCOMMON PRAYERS is arranged in such a way as to be at the service of the praying community and individual. To help highlight the spiritual insight, the inspiration and the interpretation of each poem, a short prayer has been extracted from each one and placed as an introduction, together with the corresponding scriptural text.

A variety of uses suggest themselves for this collection of poems. It certainly is a book to be enjoyed by anyone who has a special taste for poetry. It will also serve as a stimulus for private prayer and reflection. It offers special possibilities for giving texture, for adding the contemplative dimension to common prayer in small groups. Selectivity as to the appropriate poem for a particular prayer situation will always be crucial in the use of poetry for prayer.

The previously published works of Catherine de Vinck have had a profound influence on the prayer of the Weston Priory Community. It is with the hope that many other persons and communities will discover and be enriched by her poetry that this present collection is being offered. An encounter with such a poetic gift as this will bring joy to the hearts of many, and the response to its challenge will move us forward in our search to learn how to pray in our times.

Brother John Hammond
Weston Priory, O.S.B.
1976

*Give me another day, Lord :*
*evening, morning, noon*
*tomorrow will be a season*
*of daffodils, of beauty*
*yellow in the grass.*

## RENEW MY SPIRIT

"I, for myself, appeal to God and he saves me; evening, morning, noon, I complain, I groan; he will hear me calling" (*Ps 55:16-17*).

EVENING, morning, noon
I complain, I groan.
On axles of bones, the body's machine moves
propelled by the wish to go
from here to—where?
Destiny, destination: the wheel turns.
Eternity pumps blood into the veins
arranges the cosmos pleasantly:
the toy-mountain slopes to the village;
the little white houses have brooms
in the hands of little women: they sweep
time's honored dust
return it to the rising wind.
Cycles are never broken
that send mourners to the streets
ring glad bells over the newly born.

I complain, I groan, make lists of black woes:
ants in the sugar, bugs in the flour
solitude turning to loneliness
sticking to the skin
like a dress impossible to peel.
Of dreams I had my share:
daisy-white and tulip-red, they popped
in the air like tired balloons.
Who sold them to me? Who was the vendor
by the fountain in the park?
Spring returns, yes, to stretch green webs

over old trees, but the poor and the dead
are always with us: they sit on the benches
nodding, flaunting their rags
in April's leafing light.
The bread I chew does not defeat my hunger
and all the fire I own is one blue ring
flame enough to heat a cup of rain.

I complain, I groan, lift
my wooden bowl, my open beggar-palms.
The crumbs on the floor are for mice and crickets.
Am I not more than a sparrow
and in need of more gold
than the proverbial lily?

Give me another day, Lord:
  evening, morning, noon
  tomorrow will be a season
  of daffodils, of beauty
  yellow in the grass.

*Lord, I thirst:*
*disguised, an animal mask clamped*
*over my face, I come with spirit-thirst*
*to your shoreless flowing.*
*I come by night*
*to these dark unknown waters*
*and lap the infinite freshness of you.*

# My Soul Thirsts for God

"As a deer longs for running streams, so longs my
soul for you, my God. My soul thirsts for God; the
God of life" (*Ps 42:1-2a*).

A small cup held under a faucet
    I collect what streams
from imagined hills?
How far the source
    first moisture
    on the earth's porous skin?
On the hand, a water-print;
in the mind, a twisting like a cold snake
    a thin river of words
    quivers and foams.

I drink
    I thirst
    drink bucketfuls
    torrents, lakes
    dream-waters rising
    from deep unconscious wells.
I drink and still thirst.

The river fills with swimming creatures
images, fish-populations, swarms
of pressing bodies.
It is the beginning of time:
I stand on the shore of a great astral sea.
Stars are copper pennies jingling in my pocket;
these waters are still
by which I stare into a night
wider, more luminous than the sun.

I drink
but even as I lift it
bring it to my lips
the cup shatters: cold shards enter my life
slash like savage knives
the roots of my wishes.
   I thirst
with a pain I cannot hold.
And what am I:
        mere rising vapor
        no one can change?
        A water-charged mist
        no one can turn
        into the blessedness of flood?

Lord
   I pull weight
   —bones and body—
   through the tortuous practice of a will
      seeking
not words cast in the shape of raindrops
not cupped signs to catch the melting snow
but
   the torrent of your eyes
   the streaming of your truth.

Lord, I thirst:
   disguised, an animal mask clamped
   over my face, I come with spirit-thirst
   to your shoreless flowing.
      I come by night
   to these dark unknown waters
   and lap the infinite freshness of you.

Have mercy on me
   have mercy on these small gestures
   that give love, beg recognition.
      Cover me
   with the shawl of prayer
   and let my tears come to you
   heavy and luminous as stars.

## COVER ME WITH THE SHAWL OF PRAYER

"No, I shall not die, I shall live and declare the
works of the Lord" (*Ps 118:17*).

I speak to you:
my mouth breathes
    the first letter of your ancient name
    forms the sound of forgotten words.
I speak
    but less clearly than stones
    and with less excellence than rain.
I am flesh of your flesh
    measured, poured out and recaptured
    in this cup of space
    this goblet of time.
I share with others straw bed
    and hard pillow
    the casual babble of the world
    the multiple passages
    through which the mind
    —that poor dumb fish—
    swims in search of you.
My body moves, not a blind shell, house
    of spirit lighter than my bones
    but a landscape of life:
    face, breast, knee pressed
    to the quivering ground
        I feel
    the dance of your footsteps
        shaking to life
    dead wood and frozen spring.

Have mercy on me
    have mercy on these small gestures
    that give love, beg recognition.
      Cover me
    with the shawl of prayer
    and let my tears come to you
    heavy and luminous as stars.
What is this web I meet
    this net of mist
    through which I see beyond sight?
Visible
    among invisible threads
    I struggle to force a way
    of milk and light
    to touch the source of you.

Break open, reach, lift:
    my words are bells sewn
    around ankles and wrists:
    they ring, they call.
But only death has power, hook and crook
    to haul me over the last wall:
    one sweet leap, one final cry
    and the voice drowns
        the blood rests.

*Lord, release the flow of the real*
*and tell me how to bear it*
*what muscle to use*
*what power to sharpen and shape;*
*and by your good fire*
*receive this winter child.*

## MAKE ME A PATH

"For Zion was saying, 'The Lord has abandoned
me, the Lord has forsaken me.' Does a woman for-
get her baby at the breast, or fail to cherish the son
of her womb?" (*Is 49:14-15*).

IN the family album, a child
   aged two, bundled in wool:
I stood against a painted screen
   a fakery of perpetual summer.
What has changed? I touch
   the fallacy of the day.
The world is flat
   and of coldness everlasting.
The moon shines low, scrapes
   the window with a translucent nail;
   the wind wanders, plumps the night
   like a pillow full of air.
I am alone
   locked in the lying smile of the room:
   Lazarus in the rock
   sucking death's milk
   wearing death's dirty shawl.

Lord
   why hast thou forsaken me
   left me in mutiny and pain
   the knot around my neck tighter
   and looser the words that puff
   out of my mouth?
I am a native of the rock
   a satellite of the dying sun.
How long, by childish time, shall I stand

patient and still in the corner of the photograph?
In a new year, if you will
I shall find the weather
—rain or shine—sweet to my skin.
Make me a way out of the stone
   a spiral staircase
   a bridge of suspended hope.
Make me a path
   link my frozen world
   to living branches and calling birds
   —wild swans, peacocks and larks
   to dazzle the mind's dark halls.

Lord, release the flow of the real
   and tell me how to bear it
   what muscle to use
   what power to sharpen and shape;
and by your good fire
         receive the winter child.

*Lord, I have labored all night*
*and caught nothing but ghosts on my hook.*
*Give me the power to hold each thing*
*named, naked and true.*
*I am singing to you:*
*Fill my hands with the strength*
*of all that struggles and survives*
*the ice age, the long waiting, the winter snow.*

# FEED ME

"Happy are those who hunger and thirst for what is right: they shall be satisfied" (*Mt 5:6*).

**H**UNGER, I decide it is hunger
that pulls me into the open
sets me running on the same track.
Bare branches weave a cage
for birds and sun: bright feathers
over screeching winter throats, no song.
        I hunger
leaf through books, stare at the images
stored in the dark of my head
—a beach with nets and baskets, fish-full.
Is the catch all I need
the fire, the wine-flask, the moon
silver-wetting the sea?

Time flows at my back
pressing me into the channel
of this water-clock to arrive
to meet the night with the light
of my eyes flashing on and on.
By the dream-pool, the lion will come
with the bear and the bull to print
the star-map in the sky. I sleep
wake to a different morning
but what does it mean?
The letters dance crazily in the air
drunk on imprecision and mythology.

All that is harvested and stored
laid on table and cloth slowly turns
to stink and rot.
Death is a fruit-fly in the pantry
moth in the wool, wild cell in the skin.
I fall through time's ring saying peace
peace, puffing the word to life
to fire with my cold breath.
I run, yet never leave
and what I am follows me
through the long stony rest
the dreaming of the flesh into dust.

Lord, I have labored all night
and caught nothing but ghosts on my hook.
Give me the power to hold each thing
named, naked and true.
I am singing to you:
Fill my hands with the strength
of all that struggles and survives
the ice age, the long waiting, the winter snow.

*You*
　　*my hunter*
　　*lift me now*
　　*ease me out of time.*
*With your left hand, gather me*
　　*make speed to kingdom come*
　　*make life, make fire*
　　*to spark the turning wheel:*
*They burn, the days, centuries, ages!*
*With colors of amber*
　　*blues of precious gems*
　　*the joyous red of roses*
*time burns*
*and a new earth rises*
*and a new greening.*
*With your right hand*
　　　　　　　　*hold me!*

# HOLD ME WHEN I DIE

"His left hand is under my head and his right embraces me" (*Ct 8:3*).

INSIDE the time fixed
by ornate calendars
I am knotted to earth
tangled in water-nets
in all that is here and now
tied up, caged
under soft walls of air.
Each minute knocks
against my breastbone
knife-sharp, hard as rock.
As I tend fire and lamp
I see the ruined wood vanish
in the teeth of the flame
and the light feebly draw
a ring, a small golden pool
in the inexhaustible night.
Winter.
        Snow melts on the tongue
        in thin communion flakes.
The hungry eye opens, scans the distance:
the hungry mind seeks past the ragged trees
        hunts in the white forest
        where the dream-deer browse.

God
    I pause and wonder:
    am I not sought more than I seek
    and are you not the hunter
    I the cowed prey
    trembling in the dark?

34

If I could speak my heart
spill my cup of words
scream my wildest wishes
it would all be the same
ever the same banging door
blind windows, the light's energy ebbing
and I, heavy with sleep, turning
to silence, to shadow saying
"Late, it is late!"
as I pull over my hungry eyes
great blankets of clouds
quilts of soothing snow.

God
    on my hair I wear crystal circlets
    white thorns pressed into my skull.
    It is winter, remember?
    Nails are white diamonds
    sacraments of white pain, white fire.
Breathlessly, I lie
    between past and future
    death clamped on the face
    a mask carved in ice and stone
    by a million patient years.

You
    my hunter
    lift me now
    ease me out of time.
With your left hand, gather me
    make speed to kingdom come
    make life, make fire
    to spark the turning wheel:
They burn, the days, centuries, ages!
With colors of amber

blues of precious gems
  the joyous red of roses
time burns
and a new earth rises
and a new greening.
With your right hand
         hold me .

*We praise you, Lord*
*for our rooted feet:*
*by the thousand*
*with sycamore and pine, we stand*
*deep in your soil. We grow*
*in halos of light*
*and in a world where nothing signals*
*but in barks and grunts and cries*
*we scratch our signs on papyrus and steel*
*we breathe measured sounds*
*and with gladness of mind and tongue*
     *say your name.*

## Bless the Lord, O My Soul

"All you who worship him, bless the God of gods,
praise him and give him thanks, for his love is ever-
lasting" (Dn 3:90).

THE ancient gods entered
the pelts of coyotes and foxes
ran disguised under the moon.
We root deep into the hills
dig the buried skulls
count teeth and length of jaws.
Where are the snows of yesteryear?
Time beats upon the door
breaks the lock of the room
where we talk, eat, touch.
With farewells of plumes and corn
the old men went underground
who painted on the rock
their alphabets of beasts.
Are we the dreams they dreamed
are we the ghosts rising in the smoke
of peace-pipe and campfire?
We multiply, move up on the ladder
—one step, then another—set our feet
upon the next plateau, hang
on the ledge of a new age.
We press and build, go home
on the five o'clock bus:
they ride with us, the long-ago people
their thoughts in our brains
their ways in our blood.
We are a multitude: the snows of yesterday
powder our hair, print our path.

Lord, in the oldest mounds
our relics, toys and toppled bones
bear less weight of history
than the fern-etched stone.
Only hours ago, we invented
the dog-faced gods, the magic of the hunt
the spearing rite.
In time's whorled chambers
in the enormous silence of the caves
our words astonish, our language rings
in silver alternance: arrivals and partings
pleasure and grief.
Yes, we hug the earth
find comfort, reprieve in the twigged shade:
the sun pricks, the stars are alien orders
but dirt under the fingernails speaks
of our estate, our coal, our grapes and wheat.

We praise you, Lord
for our rooted feet:
by the thousand
with sycamore and pine, we stand
deep in your soil. We grow
in halos of light
and in a world where nothing signals
but in barks and grunts and cries
we scratch our signs on papyrus and steel
we breathe measured sounds
and with gladness of mind and tongue
       say your name.

*I trust*
    *unknown, dark, unanswering YOU.*

# I TRUST

"The Lord is my shepherd, I lack nothing. In mead-
ows of green grass, he lets me lie" (*Ps 23:-1*).

I N the spiral place
I turn upon myself
        going nowhere:
the room around me pivots
the world circles, closes.
There is a name for this season
for this mood: I could find it
in old calendars, in the newspapers
tacked on the walls of log cabins
sunk roof-deep in northern snows.
Now
        I only hear water
        running step over stony step
        to flood the marshes
        for the returning swans.
The law of the land speaks
in short green words: two inches above ground
                        daffodils
                        the thrust of the wild lilies.
But what are those to me
when my eyes come home masked
to see the masked room:
        meaning concealed, images trapped
        and I myself caught
                        —meat in the fruit
                        seed in the shell.
Is it wonder that I fall slack
folded head to knees
wishing sleep, sleep of infancy

wet sleep of the sea?
The Lord is my shepherd.
In the pasture I only count
                 the black ciphers of crows.
                 Was the cup ever full?
                 Dreams of understanding
                 rivers of love, ambrosia
                 I drank till morning, woke
                 burdened, robbed of the taste
                 of the salt and the sweet.

It is late: time curls
into a snaked charm
     a noose in which I hang.
I trust:
     extended, my fingertips only grasp
     wispy rags
     scissored scraps of life.
I trust
     not memory or camera
     not the grey-telling smoke
     twisting from the fire's feeble hissing:
I trust
     unknown, dark, unanswering YOU.

*Lord, let us know
    the sight, sound, touch
    of resurrected life.*

# LORD, SAVE ME!

"He has snatched us from the underworld, saved us from the hand of death, saved us from the burning fiery furnace, rescued us from the heart of the flame" (*Dn 3:88*).

HIDDEN in the cave
warmed with milk
your face turned, set
      toward that distant hill
sweet Christ
      your star sings loud over us
as we button our coats
wrap our cold bones
in skins of thread.
We have heard the sound of your death:
      red flags of flame snap
      over Rome, Dresden, Moscow;
      Troy burns behind us
      —a straw torch to every man.
Through Guernica
the horsemen ride at breakneck speed.
Under the hoofs, dust clouds
the lace and ivory of women's bodies
the moon-skulls of children.

We cling to the unicorn, to the flowered hat
look through the tent's lifted flap:
Ah, the circus, the fair, the mechanical horses!
We surge on the music
      up with the tumbler and the clown
      but the crowd laughs
      the lion enters the arena
      sets its teeth to the task:

can death be this orange beast
blazing in the sand?

Sweet Lord, have mercy on us!
Our words are pebbles rinsed
in the mouth: over and again
our jaws close on the bitter crust
on the stone we chew instead of bread.
Beauty and the Beast have met
and she is going down
falling through space
dying without answers.

Sweet Christ, the door is shut
        the rock does not turn
        that blocks the cave where we lie
        rigid on cold slabs
        —spices packed in the armpits
        perfume sprayed in the air.
It is not simple:
man does not live by pain alone
but needs active verbs of joy
things moving together
each one rare, each one abundant
laced together
in the grab-bag of the four winds.

Lord, let us know
        the sight, sound, touch
        of resurrected life:
        flowing water, rising sap
        girl humming on the air waves
        —all those marvelous ladders of beings
        animal, man, angel
        going up and down
        with melodious steps.

Let us see
 beyond the daily clang
 of pots and pans and broken bones.
"Beauty will save the world"
 —is saving the world now
 emerging from the winter rains
 wet and new and singing.

Lord, I am this raw cry, this mad howling
    unleashed in the wilderness;
  I am this shaking sound
  deep in the throat of space.
Lord
    open to me
       let my cry come unto you!

# Help My Unbelief

"I do have faith. Help the little faith I have" (*Mk 9:25*).

WHO are you, speaking in the air
voice without face
sound without lips
dropping stone-words in my path?
Are you spirit of the rainfall
ghost of the late night?
Are you wooden, empty shell
through which the wind sighs;
shape stuffed with rags
wearing a grinning head
a calabash of rattling seeds?

In that middle-kingdom of silence
    —the bed still
    mirrors the only light—
I wanted to leap
    my naked feet on the floor of certitude
    lightly dancing, keeping time
    to the music in my head.
The cock's crow punctured the dream
spoke of treason: how can I begin to pray
when my very blood races away from you
when the ground trembles, sags
under the weight of my leaving?
I struggle in the dark
hands slipping, knees breaking
broken; I crawl away from you.
Skin, bones, these are my limits
walls that enclose, contain

the veins' webbing
the glowing coal of the heart.
Where is the road from here to there
the way out of this present maze?
Sharpened lines meet and cross
slashing the cloth of my life
into rags good only to mop
what seeps under the door:
shapelessness    unreality    death.
The chair turns to shadow
the desk to vapor; familiar trees
collapse; the garden
folds on silent hinges, thins
to a single crumbling leaf.

Nothing
      I wear nothing
      I for whom the world was a silken coat
      weightless upon the shoulders.
I flex fingers and toes
strike thought against thought
making fire: rage, terror, grief
these are intimations, flares
of the working mind.
But something pulls at nerve and muscle
shuts the accessible room, unravels
the knitted truth of sky and stone.
      Am I mere reflection on the water
      a passing dream in the eye of a fish?
      Am I melting with the cloud
      flowing to dissolution with the rain
      one small drop rolling
      down the slanting board of time?
Ocean of nothingness, it flows
over my head; the sun is dead

and how shall I seek, how shall I spell
a name, a form I do not know?

Lord, I am this raw cry, this mad howling
     unleashed in the wilderness;
     I am this shaking sound
     deep in the throat of space.
Lord
     I find neither shelter nor food
     no light to touch the unreachable rose
     no oil to heal the blazing wound.
The ancient loom is ruined
and stilled the hand that with the shuttle flew
from one end of the earth to the other
weaving blankets of praise
sheets printed with sacred words.
Lord
     open to me
          let my cry come unto you!

But, yes, invent my life, light
        a passionate fire
        a thing of blazing gold
and let me laugh in your joy
        my laughing God
and leap in your rising
                    my Dancer!

# TEACH ME HOW TO DANCE

"David and all the House of Israel danced before
the Lord with all their might, singing to the accom-
paniment of lyres, harps, tamburines, castanets and
cymbals" *(2 Sm 6:5)*.

LIFE is a bed of roses
    a bowl of ripe cherries—
          Ha!
Long ago the flowers curled
to a papery death
blackbirds rifled the berry-tree
mindless of cat, bell and shouting child.

In the mirror of another time
    I look
showing myself uneasy
    coming
into history, ritual, rubble
asking, "Who am I?
          What images swim
          in these sealed depths?"
In the backroom of childhood
aproned mothers sit by the fire
their knees huge, their laps
throne or cradle. Further in time
earth-mothers squat on the cave's pitted rock
pounding grain, rolling clay in their palms
fashioning the future.

Here, among dishes and cups
    I sip the nectar of roses
    eat one sweet cherry

but
      life is a hard pallet in a cold night
sometimes
          at best
             a place of white linen
a nest in which to dream the next question:
What to do? What to wear?
      Into what form to turn?
Mythologies, legends invent themselves
but I pound the words, crack their shells
cook their meat on the spit of my years.
Thus I survive
          by skill, by luck
          saved by art and grace
and I say
      God
          I delight in your work
          I have seen you in stick and stone
          my laughing God, Lord of the garden
          Father of power over seed and root.
From moment to moment
invent my life
          Lord of movement and change
          invent me.
Gather the dusty sparrows of my days
hear them sing in your eternal branching.
      Pain, exile, hunger
      the bitter rains dripping through the walls
      the house stripped
          —I do not want a bed of roses.
Grass will grow
where beam upon beam, bone upon bone
          stand now in measured connection.
          —I do not want a bowl of cherries.

But, yes, invent my life, light
        a passionate fire
        a thing of blazing gold
and let me laugh in your joy
        my laughing God
and leap in your rising
              my Dancer!

*Answer*
      *answer us, O God!*
*Return us to level ground*
*familiar houses, small altars of memory.*
*Call us*
      *if not to sunshine*
*then to a moon-striped night*
*where we can begin again*
      *picking stones one by one*
      *to build a temple.*

## Send a Message to Our Drowned World

> "Let not the flood-waters overwhelm me, nor the
> abyss swallow me up, nor the pit close its mouth
> over me" (*Ps 69:16*).

N the full moon
          if we dare to climb
the ladder of dreams, we find
not the effort of walking on chalky dust
but the signs
            readings
                charts
of what is most tangible, nearest:
birth, death, the rites of man.
Ring of the moon
          of the earth
circling birds
          water-falling of time . . . .
We spin around:
          the wheel is our sign.
Can we break out
          to another element
          a looser shape?
"We only fear;
          we fear those things which are about
          and of which we have no sure
              knowledge . . . ."
Curled head to toe
          we roll through space
          blind children
          with veins shot full of fear.
Death speeds in our blood
an arrow of dark passage whistling
through the brain.

58

We know
      neither place nor hour
      but the crows gather
      the ants begin their trek.
Answer
      answer us, O God!
——Incertitude
            doubt
                  the vagaries of the heart
become the trembling of water:
it seeps into our rooms
through keyholes and cracked glass;
a silent glittering power
it fills ears and mouth, locks
liquid curves above our head.
Send
      a message to our drowned world
hear the echoing bells of our sunken towers.
To a sun we do not see
      does the lily flower open?
      Does the prayer blaze in your sight?
We slowly sink
            face still breathing, shimmering
            but with body half-ghosted
            with dissolving mind.
We are water
            invisibly streaming
                  through the loops of your net
                  O Fisherman, Keeper of rivers and seas!

Return us to level ground
familiar houses, small altars of memory.
Call us
      if not to sunshine
then to that moon-striped night

where we can begin again
       picking stones one by one
      to build a temple.

*GIVE US FIRE!*
*Half-seen on the remote path*
*the woman wears*
*a cloak of rain*
*she weeps and shines*
*Lady of the lonely distance*
*Mother.*

## GIVE US FIRE

"A great sign appeared in the sky, a woman clothed
with the sun, with the moon under her feet, and on
her head a crown of twelve stars" (*Rv 12:1*).

THE roots of life's tree claw the earth
dig deep into the rock
move through tunnels of years
to dim and obscure chambers.
The only light: pale fire upon a stone.
Small hands guard the flame, turn
meat on a wooden spit.

Farther
        deeper than the first cave
what do we find?
                A watery womb
                life of clustered cells
                bright nebulae
                afloat in a sea the moon-goddess pulls
                back and forth
                in a samely rhythm.
We cannot forget:
                the past moves with us.
The muttering ghosts stand at our back
pressing us into a future
they have no power to shape.
Wet, gray, the clay rests in our palms
ready to be thrown on time's wheel.
What form will sing under our fingers?
What wine will flow from lips of earth
we fashion as we go?
What blessed hand will hold
the roundness of our life?

The child slides on a bannister of years
finds himself cold on the flagstones
of a room he does not quite remember:
ancient beams cross over his head
strips of darkness tie his ankles
bind his wrists. In the wall
a window appears, a slit of bubbly glass.
Beyond the pane, a path snakes out
    clear at first
      traced with great care
      then distantly blurred
      half-hidden by brambles and wild grass.

The woman on the path wears a mantle of sun:
    "Mother!" cries the child
    his mouth alive within the wall.
But his words are fur and nails, scurrying about
brown mice of sound in search of meaning.

The narrow room expands
    vines sprout from the cracking floor
    supporting green mandibles
        flat leaves
    that hoist the roof; a staircase grows
        spiraling
        into the air.
Sheeted in moonlight
we shout new phrases
invent a new life: set lamps on high shelves
        take to broom and rag
        sweep the dust;
        on the table set dish and cup.
Merchants come to the door: we buy
    enormous melons, coconuts, oranges
    spices, teas, jewels of the sea.

We eat, we drink in leisure and ease;
we paint cheek and eyelash, replace
our dying hair. Under fiber wigs
our thoughts are of straw, dry stubble.
We cannot turn:
                surfaces of angles and corners
                objects of brass, steel and wood
                      choke us;
                elegant beasts sit at our feet:
                    they are legion
                    their eyes are glowing stone
                    they are voiceless.

    GIVE US FIRE!

Around us the earth is verdant of leaves
leathery of hide, heavy of scent.

    GIVE US FIRE!

Half-seen on the remote path
the woman wears
        a cloak of rain;
        she weeps and shines
Lady of the lonely distance
                Mother.
She speaks:
        one word of fleshed flame leaps
        in the middle of time
        middle of space.
Dry are the days of our lives:
        gathered twigs, broken reeds tied
        in useless bundles.
The flaming word shouts fire in their midst.
We hold to the heat our swollen frozen hands
        as we watch our fortune melt
        in bitter clouds of smoke.
We are blinded, stripped;
        the ground burns under our feet

great blisters appear on the skin of the world.
Is this the end to which we sorrow?
Is this the last sound, that whining in the ear
    fire eating fire
                huge mouth devouring all we know?
The woman wears a tunic of gold.
"Mother!" we cry, "Lady of the blossoming heaven!"
The path has found us:
           we go home.

We need a home for love
　　a place to end all loneliness
　　to speak low, to say yes.
There will be a new earth and a new heaven.

# I BELIEVE

"Then I saw a new heaven and a new earth. The
first heaven and the first earth had disappeared"
(*Rv 21:1*).

HUNGRY, the mouth sucks
      the hand takes.
Hear the small sound of lips
      of life quietly pulsing.
We have come by the river
    over the steel bridge, holding the rail
    of a thousand days; we need shelter:
    rain needles the skin, covers
    our sleepy faces.
We need a home for love
    a place to end all loneliness
    to speak low, to say yes.

There will be a new earth and a new heaven.

I look at the river:
    dark undertow, life-currents reach me
    hook my flesh, beat
    against my walls;
    water-weeds tie my wrists and I feel
    the dizzying spell
    sea-song, ground-swell.
I hear the call and turn away, held
    by what roots, by what strength?

We remember: it is that time again.
The puzzle on the floor, broken pieces
    of sky and land, awaits our patient fingers.
In the rasp of old leaves, we hear

the breathing of past summers, remember
what the snail whispered
what the fire said:
death is not feathers and glue
a mask in the frame of the door:
it is a worm within, a set of teeth
clicking, clipping in the dark.
Our goose is cooked
our fat already drips
in the witches' brew.
What answer to that wisdom?
What anger against that final flare?

My beloved comes leaping over the hills
he enters the moving circle
dances the day alive and sweet
dances birds in the bush
fish in the stream
and the long wind in the harp of stones.
The cat's cradle of hours falls slack
and we are free: every bone in right order
sound limb, flesh immaculate
—not a speck of dust spidering the sun.

There will be a new earth and a new heaven.

Do you believe?
I do believe
even with the fading face in the mirror
dead dogs, flies on the garbage heap
mud, beetles, rot in the wound
—even with the snaking of time, its flash
and hisses, its bite, I do believe:

There will be a new earth and a new heaven.

*Open*
    *faceless house*
    *eyeless dark;*
*become gate*
        *password*
        *arch*
*through which I*
*and the world's breath*
    *can enter.*

# Open to Me

"I cry to you, Lord my Rock! Do not be deaf to me, for if you are silent, I shall go down to the pit like the rest" (*Ps 28:1*).

OPEN to me
   hard-closed shell
   domed house around which I trace
   the circle of my chant.
Flintstone struck against my substance
arrowhead flying through the eyes
of all seeing things, speeding
through my veins: you, you
wound my hands and feet
draw blood from the open heart!

Stone of God
   glimpsed only in sleep
   dream-agate, huge, phosphorescent:
   my bones melt in your light.
What man has not heard
a silence so dark and dazing
and not stepped forward, backward
to flee, to find
   road, city, room
   a life trapped
   between papered walls
   and curtained ways?
Arriving there
what does he know?
Caught in ice, the quick fish of the mind
freezes, naked flesh turns to snow.
What does he learn?
That lovers, thousands of years past

are buried in pyramids
behind masks of gold?

Within your silence
I clap my hands: do you hear
flesh against flesh, bone against bone
motion fused to sound, both raised
higher and higher, dancing
upon the rock of you?

Open to me:
    I am not content to read
    white words on the birds' throats
    on the foolish heads of flowers.
They speak clearly, purely
but I want you
    illegible black word
    hidden in the deepest folds
    of timeless wisdom.
No, I am not content to live
    wrapped in my own life:
that shirt woven of raw silk
    of delicate webbing, clings
    in a thousand threads of joy, of pain.

Not I, not I alone
    come to you
but riders of fast hopes
men, women locked in time's ring
bound with their children
and their children's children
to the movement of the moon
the gestures of the wind.
Dressed in their ribbons and wools
they come to you
    held, carried

leaning on one another
a horde of cripples
a tribe of hobbling fools.

Open
   faceless house
   eyeless dark;
become gate
        password
        arch
through which I
and the world's breath
   can enter.

*Now, Lord*
*let me see the fathering life*
   *flowing in the veins:*
   *blood and sap*
   *nourishing the world.*
*Let me see*
   *beyond what appears*
   *as sun, stars and rushing wind.*

## Let Me See the Way

"I am the Way, the Truth and the Life. No one can
come to the Father except through me. If you know
me, you know my Father too" (*Jn 14:6-7*).

IT was formed somewhere
in the lime-house of the brain
   first thought, invented image
   tool
   not of stone, wood or rag
   but weightless, of air.
I shelter it
   emerald dream, gem flashing
   green rays around my head.
What is truth? I ask
   where is the tree?
                    THERE
outside of me; I touch, smell, chew
twig and fruit, carve a name
deep in the bark. I see
   —but does the tree grow
   out of my eyes shaking
   a foolish mass of leaves?
   Or does it split the vault
   of earth and rock
   to claw its way into my mind?

First, the time, the place
then the fracas of birth: I come
   into myself, waking, hearing
   more than the banging door.
The room holds a prayer rug
   a wine cup of fired clay
   books on a dusty shelf;

and I, in my flesh coccoon
    unfold words, images, move
    like a scarab in a ring of light.

Tortuous is the way, and I come
    from afar, bearing weights
    dressed in the history, wisdom
    rite of ancient people.
Days crack open like dropped shells
nights are pools aswarm with fish:
    dream-forms impossible to catch.
Tomorrow, yes, I shall rest by sleeping fires
tomorrow the long lost clue will return
    alive and pulsing: I will remember
    the thousand years ago.

Now, Lord
    I turn to the sight
    of the paradise tree
    to the knowledge of good and evil.
Let me see the fathering life
    flowing in the veins:
    blood and sap
    nourishing the world.
Let me see
    beyond what appears
    as sun, star and rushing wind.
But save my human grip:
    the feel of the touching body
    the speaking tongue, the stepping foot.
In measured limits
    here    now
the way to boundlessness begins;
and truth is born humbly
    here    now

in reach of ear and eye:
the lips can tell
and so can the kissed face
   the fist unclenched
   the hand held.

God
   give me
          —I am mad with hunger
          stretched and curved
          to your shape and sound
  give me
          the edible diamonds of your love
          the nourishing rubies of your fire.

## I WOULD PRINT YOUR NAME ON MY TONGUE

"Between these animals something could be seen
like flaming brands or torches, darting between the
animals; the fire flashed light, and lightning streaked
from the fire. And the creatures ran to and fro like
thunderbolts" (*Ez 1:13*).

I would print your name on my tongue
    sew it in my cloak
    hold it safe in the cage of words
but you move elsewhere
    tiger
        tiger burning bright
            passing through the lock and catch
            of the blazing forest.
And I, love-blind, take
    by the quick of night
    the lonely path
    to hunt you
        tiger scented with fire
        with the terrible profound smell
        of all that burns on the spit of time.
I have prepared, touched my forehead
    painted my body with red pigment
    polished my skin with oil.
Oh, gentle of dress and speech
I enter the gateless dark
    the grove
        where
            by the pool's fine glass
    the tiger comes to drink.
Lord
    do not mark wonders in my path:
    manna crackling underfoot

flight of quail at sunrise;
in flesh and fur
        I am real
        towering over clawing roots
        lording over cloud-palaces
yet even wrecked and spilled
I want no thread or glue
    no patch of truth, no renascence
    of pain, of long and ardent wishing:
I want you
    tiger tamed, light
    in the dark places
    of all that is brotherly
    sisterly, near.
God
    beyond the words
    that are palm-fruits and pines
        bird eggs and apple seeds
give me
    who am mad with hunger
    stretched and curved
    to your shape and sound—
give me
    the edible diamonds of your love
    the nourishing rubies of your fire.

*God*
    *I ask again and again*
    *for I am this question*
    *screaming in your space:*
    *one among many, looking*
    *for the possible door, the answer*
    *carved into the ever-circling O*
    *of your peace.*

## I Hear a Manner of Answer

"I tell you, therefore: everything you ask and pray
for, believe that you have it already, and it will be
yours" (*Mk 12:24*).

ask
    and in my daily dust ask again:
Where is the way?
Does the knife know, the plow, the falling axe?
I dip the pen, begin to draw:
        beyond account, the line moves
        from a hilltop to a landscape
        of astonishing rocks.
Can I explain why the word stone
        drops on the page with a grey weight?
How the world's fragments speed
        dangerously about? Glass shards
        needles of perception  break
        the skin, enter the brain.

Changes, miracles of invention
        build new shapes, new sounds:
        among the multitudes, the swarming choices
where is the guiding cord
        the single thought uncoiled
        from the tangled mess?

Intricate, voluminous
billowing around my ankles:
        a Japanese robe, a silken wrap
        such is my life; but who sees
        my iron shoes, the dark bruise on my flesh?
At the table of the world
I take and eat

the sugar-cones of mountains
take and lift
the steaming bowl of the sea.
But I still hunger, still fear:
death is no sweet apple
but a clustered thing hung
at eye-level in the weighted tree.

God
I ask again and again
for I am this question
screaming in your space:
one among many, looking
for the possible door, the answer
carved into the ever-circling O
of your peace.
Where are those who came before me:
the people marching through sand-storms
carrying the day's provisions
a water-jar, a scroll
a pot to cook the morning manna?

It so happens: today I am stranded
among steel pipes and motor cars
—but the crows in the oak tree
are very old, and the wind
from age to age drums
the same message against the walls.
God
the oracle speaks:
your voice in pine and palm
in fish-scale and bright coral;
your prophecies
in the veins of each leaf
in bone and living face.

I hear it
    a manner of answer, a word
moving
    dark and quick
        behind the glass.

*God of the moon-age, let me explain:*
*my palms are wet, caught in terror*
*but beyond crust and bark, I hear*
*your coming, your spurs clanging*
*upon my way.*

# I AWAIT YOUR COMING

"They will see the Son of Man coming on the clouds
of heaven with power and great glory" (*Mt 24:30*).

BEYOND the shell
beyond the greenness of the green
beyond the skin that wraps
    the mummy in black leather:
silence, a descent into darkness
    a slow fall.

God of the moon-age, I touch
    and taste and set my foot
    upon your path. I am a moving speck
    on your dizzying distance
    a cinder blown across your face.
My body stands naked in the wind
    a small warm cloud rising
    from its flesh; it cries, burns
    sweats; it thrashes about, held together
    by a single idea that gathers
    assembles ribs, spine, skull:
    the frame of a creature real enough
        to die.

The world is full of marvelous roars:
    birth-sounds, love-sounds, messages
    of clapping hands, of flames
    that shoot sky-high their velvet power.
Ghosted hunters
women with bellyfull of children
former dwellers of sea and land, return
    breaking through time-waves
    fluctuating between memory and oblivion.

Their being mingles with my blood
  in a central knot of life; out of their past
  I have grown into a presence renewed
    from day to day without repetition
—each moment a universe
  that comes into light, a pod
  ripe with seeds, an exploding capsule
  rich with the milk of meaning.

God of the moon-age, let me explain:
  my palms are wet, caught in terror
  but beyond crust and bark, I hear
  your coming, your spurs clanging
    upon my way.

Where are we going?
   To dusty moon-bowls
   cradles of moon-rocks?
Here by the ancient dullness
   of earth-ache, earth-clock
Lord, refresh our long love
fill our human shell
   with new hope.

## Lord, Give Us Hope

"Those who hope in the Lord renew their strength,
they put out wings like eagles. They run and do not
grow weary, walk and never tire" (*Is 40:31*).

TIME was
     a smudged postcard
     saying love and so-long
     faking permanence while fogging
     the issues out of sight.
And time was
     a place in the past
     life nailed down
     with the beams and the roof
     of a waterless house.
We were
     morning, noon and evening;
we were clocks, the numbers flicking by
       the-hands obsessed
       in their endless turning.
Anger growls in our animal throats;
grief is
     today   tomorrow
     a sweater form-fitting our soul
     knitted from the rough fibers
     of impatience, of hunger.
Quick
   we touch
      kiss once more:
time stops, double-tracks.
The bell rings, someone stands by the door:
  a little girl selling pencils?
  Death as a black dog scratching,
  asking admittance?

We fight for memory
   for full taste and smell and sound.
Floating jellied cell
   in the primal ooze
fish with pulsing mouth
          how long ago?
Now, our skin without scale or fur
    shivers and sweats; our clothes itch.

Where are we going?
    To dusty moon-bowls
    cradles of moon-rocks?
Here by the ancient dullness
    of earth-ache, earth-clock
Lord, refresh our long love
fill our human shell
     with new hope.

*Where can we go?*
*Here*
     *in depth of rock*
        *of time*
        *of flesh*
*a child is born*
        *and we are home.*

# A Child Is Born

"For there is a child born for us, a son given to us,
and dominion is laid on his shoulders; and this is the
name they give him: Wonder-Counsellor, Mighty
God, Eternal Father, Prince of Peace" (*Is 9:6*).

W HERE can we go?
Road and mountain-pass are closed
and winter's white paws flex open
reach to claw our life away.
We moved across ice-ages
hunters following game tracks.
Under what moon did we first know
the shape of the wheel, the rolling motion
of roundness, when did we first hear
the clock's ticking and begin to forget
the alphabet of stones and stars?
Our true time is the time of the child
of the rose and of the wind.
We are wedded to movements
of planets, of waves
sea-milk and sand.
By what sunflowered path
did we descend to the landscape
of screaming wounded faces
of junkyards, of dark air
that carries the spores of death?

Where can we go? Even as we speak
language falls, weightless, wilted
words cut from their stems
left to wither on the ground.
We have come to the world's end:
our small bones, our grain and honey

call for rituals of life
long for wet earth, bees and new sun.
What answer of absolute presence
awaits us in this cave
in this dusk?
Flesh seeks out flesh, real hand, pulsing wrist
seeks to touch, hold, kiss
and tires of shallow play
of small flickering lights upon the wall.
Here
in depth of rock
of time
of flesh
a child is born
and we are home.

Past this gate, my sister, my spouse,
   you are, beyond yearning and tears
      forever beautiful
         forever signed by your lover's hand.

## ADVENT

"Open to me, my sister, my love, my dove, my perfect one, for my head is covered with dew, my locks with the drops of the night" (*Ct 5:2*).

OPEN to me, my sister, my spouse
                    my earth-house, my gate!
Within ruined walls
                    music plays:
        concert of colors and shapes
                    of street-bells and horns
        cymbals of the ashcans
        drumbeat of heels
                    upon the skin of time.


And it comes to pass:
        the blind body begins to stir
        to dance
                    out of its darkness
        to see diagrams, signs
                    whole webs of sun and sky
                    looped into a single meaning.
What voice speaks
        in the light of fire
                    whip of rain?
What heaviness, what memory moves
        in the blood? The past rises:
lips of a thousand buried mouths
        sing anew: hands cross boundaries
                    reach out
        their flesh grafted over old bones
                    alive again and warm.

Open to me, my sister, my spouse
        my earth-house, my dream!

Wandering over dry grass
wondering who will sell or lend
    a shelter: house of sticks
    of mud to the great Traveler?
No room at the inn
    but wide space under the stars
    infinite vastness unlocking
    in the smallest seed
    and distances untold, undreamed
    in the natural heart.

They call it world
        this web of stone and clay
        this cave of whispering dark.
Never room enough to spread
        to stretch legs, life, song.
Yet, it comes to pass:
        through the narrow door
    in ancient wind-swept dust
a new flesh begins to stir
        to dance all things
        alive and free.

Past this gate, my sister, my spouse
you are, beyond yearning and tears
    forever beautiful
    forever signed by your lover's hand.

Call me, Lord, with my thirsty sisters
     to the coolness of that place
     to all that moves, tips down
     speaks wet and sings.

# OUT OF THE DESERT, CALL ME

"They shall not hunger or thirst, nor shall the
scorching wind or the sun strike them; for he who
pities them leads them and guides them beside
springs of water" (*Is 49:10*).

I N the long wandering
              I woman
in the dry wandering of my kind
came by chance, not by will
    into the desert
—Heat and prickly pears
    the thorns in my needy hands.
It is high noon.
The wind's delirium raises cities of sand
the stones burn.

    —God, send me a well
      a cup of rain
      one drop on my tongue.

White, copper or black
they wander, the women, my sisters
    in their ring of birth.
They move from place to place
    house to street to car
the burden in their hips alive
a lumpy word they understand.

I myself with new child on my knee
—son of my son, one-year-old man—
hear their voices:
they come like water rushing over rocks
        wetting the world: mothers
    breast-heavy, offered.

The young mouths, the sucking lips
take and drink.

          Milk in the desert
          the honey of women.

I heard:
      somewhere in oases of weather
      the earth is soft, broken
      by hard green thrusts.

I heard
      of water falling white and smoky
      from stony ledges
      gathering below to stream anew.

Call me, Lord, with my thirsty sisters
      to the coolness of that place
      to all that moves, tips down
      speaks wet and sings.

*How long*
*before the pines' sap, drop*
*by sweet drop, becomes solid amber?*
*How long before my life dripping*
*through days and nights, takes*
*translucent shape through which*
*your light can flow?*

# I EAT, I DRINK

"All that came to be had life in him and that life
was the light of men, a light that shines in the dark,
a light that darkness could not overpower" (*Jn
1:4*).

WHERE are you?
Lost and found in a world
    where you are food on the table
    calling to my hunger
    ardent coal on the grate, diffusing
    warmth and light.
Nothing moves when I ask:
"Where are you?"—The fixed objects
    of the room placidly stand
    their atoms firmly assembled
    to define chair, bed, lamp.
But I move out of my depth
    out of the dark pulsing of the mind.
I run ahead of time
    into the sun's geography
    your homeland.

Your body is in the leaf
    and in the rock, in what is changing
    dying and being reborn. How long
    before the pines' sap, drop
    by sweet drop, becomes solid amber?
    How long before my life dripping
    through days and nights, takes
    translucent shape through which
    your light can flow?
I eat you now: the bread on the plate
is your body and the red coals
that warm my bones, your blood.

Lord,
   save these human faces
   which darkly rise behind the glass.

# Through the Looking Glass

"For now we see through a glass, darkly; but then face to face: now I know in part; but then shall I know even as also I am known" (*1 Cor 13:12*).

TEARING the seamed garment
we tremble within
                    ragged earth-pelt
                    sky-changing cloth.
No place could be colder
no star more removed from the sun.
Squared off, the light from the window
        loses density
                    brings no fire.
Being here
        where time moves
we touch the turning wheel.
We, in accord with noon and midnight
                count its turn.
Around a soft marrow
            wooden rings expand:
the tree rises
            sending out signals of leaves
but neither through skin nor bark
can the prisoned spirit go
                    free and easy
                    ballooning in the air.

Is there a gate, iron work
        or latched door? Can we find a clue
to read the telegrams written in stone
        by the nails of lichen
                the needles of rain?

"Mirror, mirror on the wall,
    who is the fairest of them all?"
Through the looking-glass, we fall
    with the water-falling of time.
Age strips the body we own
    in mortal fear, in hunger.
Eye socket, cheekbone, the hairless skull:
    we are fixed, transfixed by that mystery.
The sea of tranquility lies elsewhere
    in moon-dust no one shall ever scoop.
It is here
        wearing our masks
        our patched coats, that we seek
    what lies beyond the darkening pane:
        in the silvered distance
        tiny figures recede
                going  going  gone
                nowhere.
Young, we immensely begin
    to see, touch, taste the earth
    as salt and bread. How do we become deaf
    to the prophecies uttered
    even by dust and trampled grass?
Broken bones in the pit,
shards of hand-mirrors
in which time streams and ends:
seven years, bad luck; seven millenia
bad luck; the meat spoils
the worm of death works under the stone;
    there is pain
    the fruit ripens and rots
but the spilled seed shouts good news:
    life bears itself further
    beyond visible forms.

Overnight
the sticky box springs open:
animals, plants take deep breaths
the child renews these million years
      with a single cry.
There is a bridge somewhere
from lip to lip
voice to voice
from our dying
          Lord
              to your life:
a shuttle casting across the chasm
      a thread of light.

Fold the seamed cloth
—bandages and burial cloth—
We struggle
        to stand
           upright.
Lord
     save these human faces
     which darkly rise behind the glass.

*What I see when the curtains part*
*that cover the face of the abyss:*
*Mother-light*
*Father-light*
*God!*

## GIVE US LIGHT

"Make no mistake about this, my dear brothers: it
is all that is good, everything that is perfect, which
is given me from above: it comes down from the
Father of all light" (*Jas 1:17*).

IN the country of the absurd
in the dream—a wintering
    of sticks and stones, place
    of smoke and dark seeing—
I turn with the spiraling line.
No time   no time:
        coiled around my flesh
        a narrowing strip of days;
        hours squeezed in the fist
        the light colder
        and the night formless.
Nine lives scattered to the wind
nine seeds flung into an arc
    parachute to the ground of another spring
    saying:
        "Break open, put out new roots
        claim the field of changes."

Close at hand
    runs the thread of water
    to be lifted to the lips, pulled
    through the network of the soul.
I drink rivers and streams
    take all the rains into my thirst.
It is not enough: clouds pass
    over the sun, each one an angel
    a feathered turbulence swollen
    with good news. They break overhead

drench me with wet words, needle
my brain with fresh rhythms.
Do I alone with dog and owl
hear the song of the grass
suffused with green music?
Do I alone feel no joy
in the dance of the moon-hunters?
Their rocks cannot speak the stories
common pebbles tell that shine
brighter than constellations
in the path of the living.

That curved, delicate line
ahead of me
            —lonely trail of my ninth hour—
it calls, compels me to break camp
forfeit what is now habit and tool:
kettle to whistle in the dawn
mop to wipe life's overspill.
Another journey, another death.
Is this the perpetual way
    —from moment to moment
one time-zone slipping into the next
changing, turning, moving closer
to the center where the line curls
upon itself, a noose holding me still
leaving no room for blood or breath?
Is this all, is this the end?
Little phrases glued to the tongue
the body covered with solemn signs
a black flag at the gate screaming:
pestilence   ravage   flight?
The field whitens
      into clouds of flowers
      born of the one seed
      last of the nine that fell

in brambles and pockets of rock.
I am witness
        to the form of myself:
        hand    eye    color of the mind
        changes from desert to deep-throated day
        singing in the green light
        of newly-risen grass.
I am witness
        to the first image:
        speed of the time-spiral hurled
        from age to age like a spinning sun.
The crumbling stone lies;
the bloodless lips tell not the whole truth:
I am trying to write it
        with hand-print    body-print
        nativity of words.
What I see
        when the curtains part
        that cover the face of the abyss:
        not terror, not mad pulse of engines
        not dying numerals of the clock
                    but
        pure freedom    pure embrace
        the sum of all that leaps alive
                from the blind human canvas
                from sand-paintings and masks
                from calligraphs, brush-strokes
                art and wonder of the race
                        all merging, all intensified
                        all solved
                in the shine of the one great magical light
    Mother-light
            Father-light
                    God!

Father of rivers and frost
Father of birds, of children, of yes:
   we have heard the dust crying out
   and the sap of our life shouting
   louder and far beyond our death.

## Death Has No Power

"The Lord says this: Come from the four winds, breath; breathe on these dead; let them live!" (*Ez 37:9*)

OUT of its northern cave
    the wind blows, full-cheeked
        breathes ice on every earth-fold
            on every crease of stone.
In our small web of flesh
    our bones tremble: we shake, draw back
    remember warmth of womb, shelters
    where constant fires keep watch.

Are we speaking? Words congeal in the air
    hang in white balloons of breath.
With our care and our seeking
    we wish to say: "All things are well;
    the day is a plaything, a rubber ball
        bouncing on concrete, a reality
        of living equilibrium, repose and leap."
But we move with such speed, hurled
    forward from one winter to the next;
our eyes like headlights probe the dark
    looking for clues. If greenness is to come
    we should hear the speech of roots
    the underground travail of springs
    the whispers of the dead.

What is it that we wish with such sighs
    such pain, such wildness of the mind?
Love, yes, love ascending
    through all the shapes of our dying
        —fearful thoughts nightly scuttle

back and forth, tarnish the moon
spoil the bread, sour the wine.
The northern wind seeps into cracks
nails doors shut, blows lights out
one by one. But we are here:
we are now, our gloved fingers hold
the hourglass through which time shifts
and falls—and we laugh:

Father of rivers and frost
Father of birds, of children, of yes:
we have heard the dust crying out
and the sap of our life shouting
louder and far beyond our death.

*O Love,*
*        I am here, actual*
*in the midst of this nowhere*
*that is You, and my eyes see*
*the glory of the Lord.*

## My Eyes See the Glory of the Lord

> "Now, Master, you can let your servant go in peace,
> just as you promised; because my eyes have seen
> the salvation which you have prepared for all the
> nations to see, a light to enlighten the pagans and
> the glory of your people Israel" (*Lk 2:29-32*).

YEARS I spent searching
    through the green wood and the dry!
I was a child, playing
    in the nursery of the world
            arranging letters to spell
            earth    body    sun—words
            without link, broken designs
            separated from each other
            by rifts wider than the sea.

Now I go hungry, grow sleepless
    and time knots its rope
    around my neck. Dangling free
    hanging by a thread, my life
        miraculously endures.
The music in my head, the rattle
    of pebbly rimes, the bells
    tied to my ankles distract
    the birds, but hardly move
    the bones of the dead.
To survive, I must blindly
touch the seamless web
be present to the fullness
    I can only guess in distance
                in nearness.

The best month may be
     not hot and leafy June, but, who knows
     turning to ice and stone, December
     moving cold hands over the face
     of mountains, erasing all tracks.
Dark and improbable is the way
     of toil and lonely shifting.
In the sack, bread crust, tin cup, matches:
     hope enough to persist
     on the steep and windy trail.

O Love
     I am here, actual
in the midst of this nowhere
that is You, and my eyes see
the glory of the Lord.

Always
  around me
    above me
 he sets up the tent
     holds
 a canopy of peace.

## I Am Sheltered

"The angel of the Lord pitches camp round those who fear him; and he keeps them safe. How good the Lord is—only taste and see! Happy the man who takes shelter in him" (*Ps 34:7-8*).

E is there
　　　—around me
　　　　　　above and beyond—
the angel of the Lord:
a good workman in overalls and sandals
　　　he pitches the tent wherever I am:
　　　poles deep in the ground
　　　ropes tied with all the proper knots.
In a child's view of his power
　　　he is colored gold, swims in the air.
To me, he wears
　　　a collage of faces and looks:
　　　grins like a boy
　　　deep-sees, eyes in the sun, knowing
　　　in what order and rhythm
　　　the atoms dance to form
　　　tree-shapes, the leaf's sap.
I meet him often
　　　in coffee-shops, airports, on the beach:
always
　　　　around me
　　　　　　above me
he sets up the tent
　　　　　　holds
a canopy of peace.

*God, you hold me with steady grip.*
*I turn and twist, change shape:*
*Dark, dark my wishing*
*    darker than your skill:*
*I meet you everywhere.*
*"God knows!" My tongue licks these words*
*    and finds them sweet.*

# GOD KNOWS

"If I go eastward, he is not there; or westward—still I cannot see him. If I seek him in the north, he is not to be found, invisible still when I turn to the south. And yet he knows of every step I take" (*Jb 23:8-10a*).

UNDERFOOT, depth of earth
> buried silver and broken pots
> —the maize without life
> and dried the squash blossoms.
It is dark in this place:
> the light-switch is out of reach
> and time sifts, black and cold
> through long and empty tunnels.
Once, I shook the gourd, rattled the seeds
> and from a flute of bones pulled
> the owl's screech, the serpent's hissing.
Once, the century-carp in the weedy pond
> brought me messages. "I believe,"
> I said when its O mouth pulsed
> above the waterline. Now I sleepwalk
> > toward morning.
Do I dream myself alive
> a fish in weedy tangle
> a bird probing the air
> a dog scratching in a muddy yard?
Or am I woman
> mother of plenty in a house full of grain?

God, you hold me with steady grip.
I turn and twist, change shape:
> small one moment
> a worm in its sand-castle

128

huge the next
and formless like the wind.
The world's edge, the night's farthest cave
    offer no hiding: you are wound
    around the substance of all things
    and I touch you, maddening Lover
    in every curve and ring.
I am ambushed by every eye
    trapped by every pebble.
If I scream, the sound
    rubber-balls against the sky
    and brings me back your voice.
Dark, dark my wishing
    darker than your skill:
I meet you everywhere.
    —What space do you find in dust-flecks?
    What pleasure in the pistons and pipes
    of the world's machinery?
"God knows" is a common spell
the race speaks when no one can explain
    hunger, the squall in the sea's mouth
    the burning rage of doom.
"God knows!" My tongue licks these words
    and finds them sweet.

*There is nothing to say*
*except yes, Lord, we are sinners*
    *and come to pray:*
*"Have mercy on us, O God*
    *in your goodness, in your great tenderness*
*wipe away our faults."*

# Have Mercy on Us

"Have mercy on me, O God, in your goodness, in your great tenderness, wipe away my faults; wash me clean of my guilt, purify me of my sin" (*Ps 50:1-2*).

IN dark flashes, images fall
melt in a rushing stream
—fire or flood, we do not know.
Dressed in fallacies and frills
we stand by the window, rubbing our eyes.
Colors drain from the morning sun;
the garden turns black that yesterday
was painted with pink roses.

What is left? Amplified sounds
scurrying rats in tapestries of garbage
echoes of upturned pebbles.
In terror, the heart shrinks
to a pulsing red dot.
Shall no crow with bread in beak appear
no angel descend with pitcher and loaf?
—Habacuc of the stolen pot
where are you with your soup?
We starve in the dark pit, weep
find no companion but the rising wind.
There is nothing to say
except yes, Lord, we are sinners
and come to pray:
"Have mercy on us, O God
in your goodness, in your great tenderness
wipe away our faults."

*I will love you*
    *from distance to distance*
    *from star to star*
    *from beginning to beginning.*

## You Touch Me and I Live

"I say this prayer to you, Lord, for at daybreak you listen for my voice; and at dawn I hold myself in readiness for you, I watch for you" (*Ps 5:3*).

EACH morning as I wake
I inhale not air alone
    but sea and land, breathe
    stone-dust, pollen
house the world in my lungs:
    roads not traveled
        by foot or wheel
    but secretly traced
        of moonlight and waves.

Each morning as I wake
    —the garden pleasantly rings the room—
my throat burns, my palms reach out
    begging; tea steams in porcelain cups
    bread rests on white cloth
but I hunger, I thirst: my body
    turns and twists, nailed
    to images of impossible yearnings.
I fear, knowing the heart weak
    trembling before the spell.
What if I were left behind, child
    of a lost tribe without wonder
    of word? What if the salt-lick
    loses its flavor, if the tongue
    forgets the taste of light?

I was hungry and you fed me
    from that garden planted with rime
    and right reason; from a green place

where speech first sang, you brought me
full baskets and heaping trays.
From the sea's long swell
from its hauling power
you let the tide come in: new life
milky-white Venus-skin, mine
mine with the good fruit
the succulence of love.
You hold mystery to my lips
say "Drink," and blood runs
from my wrists, the joyous redness
the spill of all sweet giving.

You call me forth: I easily blend
into space, take color, shape
of weed, cloud, tree:
See my hair brushed by the wind
my fingers like branches
my toes in the mud like roots.
You shake clay from my bones
set me upright on healthy feet
send me—my head clear like a bell
ringing with your voice—
on steep and rocky paths.
You touch me, and lo, I am water
become stream, flood and overflow;
the desert fills with sounds, shakes
with rain-stars and diamonds.
You touch me, and I come
into a form of grain, of seed-ripeness
globe of the grape, wheat-head
heavy with the emblems of summer.
Take and eat! Take and drink!

I will love you
     from distance to distance
     from star to star
     from beginning to beginning.

*I weep to God: may the greening spirit*
*come to dazzle me alive*
*out of my water-sleep*
*out of my grave!*

## COME, SPIRIT OF GOD

"When you send forth your Spirit, they are created,
and you renew the face of the earth" (*Ps 104:30*).

I am still
　　with the stillness, not of stone
　　but of bird stunned
　　after a long flight.
Heap of feathers, fistful of flesh
　　that's all I am this morning
　　as the dull sound of rain wets
　　my soul
—to the raven's beak
to the hunter's net, a prey
　　without price or profit.

From high trees, the shape of my life
　　hangs with the rain's threads:
　　a coarse robe, a penitent's shirt.
Is there any taste for the tongue
　　in the bitter crust of the wind?
　　Any friendship for the eye
　　that meets the wreck of winter?
If I turn to the mirror, what rises
　　but my twin and clouded self, drowning
　　in the glass' watery depths?

The clock ticks, the hands move
　　without pause or respite
　　over the surface of space.
Yet, this moment is stilled, held
　　between two suspended waves:
　　the past frozen in jagged peaks
　　and the future ready to crash

to drop on my shoulders
with the weight of death.
Grief moves through my bones
burns me to lime and ash:
I am not woman but snail, wet worm
pinned upon dark wood.

I weep to God: may the greening spirit
come to dazzle me alive
out of my water-sleep
out of my grave.

*Over the flooded fields of sorrow*
*within the pattern of change*
*Master of the Lake, Lover*
   *you move, breaking and reassembling*
   *directions and passages*
   *casting your net*
   *reaching*
      *my deepest home.*

## Reach My Deepest Home

"Cast your net off the starboard side" he suggested,
"and you will find something." So they made a cast,
and took so many fish they could not haul the net
in (*Jn 21:6*).

ASTER of the Lake
         Boatman
     pushing your oars among the reeds
I have not seen your face.
You are word
         day-word
         way of the crossing time.
Sunrays branch out of your eyes
     enter the room I keep.
I dwell deep
     at the root of the lake:
rain pours in at the window
     its endless sound fills the living space
     where I lift water-hands towards you.
Tangled as I am
     in the shade of ancient weeds
weighted as I am with bones and blood
I cannot touch you.
In the household of the rain
     where all things stream and tremble
I wait for release: my body cold, lonely
     my spirit turning with the earth, turning.

Master of mysteries, in your net
     the stories   legends   songs of men
     born of a million years of flux
           connect
     shore to shore

continent to continent
    man to woman.
I rise to the surface, breathing
    making mine the speech of rain-bubbles and wind.
Lures dangle at eye-level:
    feather and fly
    star-shape, spangled disk:
they dance in the air
while you dip the oars, plow the waves
    open a water-road before my thirst.

Some say birth, death
    appear, disappear, reflections
    in the cloudy mirror
    in the gleaming stone
    of imagined world, of inverted dream.
But I am ringed round
    by years of greening gardens
    shaken by time's elements:
        memories, chilling hours
        bells and chants of the future.
The warmth I begin to feel
    is of real presence: curve of arm
    enchantment of the heartbeat.
Leaves, rain and wind speak to me
    an ascending language:
Over the flooded fields of sorrow
within the pattern of change
Master of the Lake, Lover
    you move, breaking and reassembling
    directions and passages
    casting your net
    reaching
        my deepest home.

*Look   see   touch*
*GOD!*

## I Try to Speak

"O Lord, our Lord, how glorious is your name over
all the earth! Out of the mouth of babes and suck-
lings you have fashioned praise" (*Ps 8:2-3a*).

AWAKE and listening
   —moonrays drilling the dark —
I try to speak: What words
   can we cry? What is given to us?
Meager alphabet, sounds
   warmth of body-language.
How to say God? I have fallen
   in love with the bleeding roots
   of his life, and I am shaken
   and loosened from my sleep.

It is late in the year: words
   in their ripe innocence, burst
   around me like seeds. If we don't hear
   their resonance, hear them
   clear through our brain, veins, flesh
   what about that other name, God?
How can it leap alive
   out of the tomb of dead signs?

From rain-wet leaves
from swollen streams, a modulation rises:
   each note singular, equal to itself.
Let no one alter or embellish
   the meaning of water
Let it be this cool, instantaneous thing
   this flow that enters the mind
   sweet and quick: look   see   touch:
      WATER!

146

The real trees have disappeared
        —stolen in the night—
while our thoughts
        kept their image safe and still:
        a green and gauzy dream, fixed
        in the middle distance
        a symmetry of sentinels, guarding
        familiar land.
Their real branches
        scrape our walls, stand
        thick, beautiful and scented
        around our lives
—yet no one stops
        to look    see    touch
                TREES
        with glossy heads roaring
        in the conflagration of the wind.

I try to speak, I, in touch
        with the earth, willing to wash
        the eyes that have lost sight
        of all that is by itself
        pure visibility. Let nothing be
        hidden: look    see    touch
        deformity of bark, sickness in the bone
        the released strictness of death.

So be it, deaf ear, bloodless heart.
Yet, the shape of death is a stone
        that falls through infinite space
        gathers speed, begins to whistle
        a deathless song.

How to say God? How, with tongue
        and feeble musical skill, to form
the syllable of his name

if the wind sleeps, retracted
like dormant snail
in a shell of blindness?
How to say God? The bleeding roots
of his life grow to full and greening wood.
Look    see    touch
GOD!

Three thousand copies
set in twelve point Times Roman with Italic
by A & S Graphics, Inc. of Wantagh, NY
and printed by
William J. Mack Co. of North Haven, CT
constitute
the
SECOND PRINTING